EXQUISITE

The Poetry and Life of Gwendolyn Brooks

by SUZANNE SLADE   illustrated by COZBI A. CABRERA

Abrams Books for Young Readers

NEW YORK

Gwendolyn grew up in the big city of Chicago with little money to spare.

Yet her family owned great treasure—
a bookcase filled with precious poems.

Each night, her father read fine poetry aloud,
passionate and proud.
Nothing sounded sweeter to Gwendolyn
than Father's deep voice
reciting the rhythmic words.

Gwendolyn memorized those lines—
fine words in time
to share with her big-hugging aunts.

When she was seven,
Gwendolyn began arranging words into poems of her own.

One day, her mother found those scribbly lines
and announced with sincere conviction
(as mothers do when making a prediction),
"You are going to be the *lady* Paul Laurence Dunbar."
Gwendolyn beamed. He was her favorite poet!

Gwendolyn loved to sit on her big back porch
with colorful clouds dancing overhead
and dream about her future—

"I was at my happiest, sitting out on the back porch,
to sit there and look out at the western sky
with all those beautiful changing clouds
and just to dream about the future,
which was going to be ecstatically exquisite,
like those clouds."

Writing became like eating and breathing to Gwendolyn—
it was something she just had to do.

She carefully strung words together like elegant jewels
in perfect meter and time.

Her rhythmic lines described paper dolls and ticktock clocks,
raindrops, sunsets, and climbing rocks.

She poured her poems into notebooks—
filled them to the very tops.
Her room became a swelling sea of poems.

When Gwendolyn turned eleven,
she decided to set her words . . .

free...

and mailed four prized poems to a newspaper.

Her words were printed on crisp pages
for the whole neighborhood to see.

Elated, she sent her nature poem "Eventide" to a magazine.
It appeared on shiny pages
for the entire country to read!

Gwendolyn's future seemed as bright as morning's first clouds.
But then a terrible storm blew in—
the Great Depression.

With too few jobs
for too many workers,
her father's pay was cut in half.
Dinner each night was the same: beans.

Hungry for food
yet more hungry for words,
Gwendolyn kept writing.

She sent more poems to magazines,
but they were all rejected.

In high school Gwendolyn felt rejected, too.
She was too quiet and shy for some crowds,
her skin too dark for others.

Every year she tried a different school—
all white,
all Black,
and a mix of both.
But she didn't seem to fit in anywhere.

Gwendolyn felt invisible.

But when words flowed from her pen,

she became invincible.

So she spent more time than ever writing,

exploring new ways to express her ideas.

She even wrote a history report in rhyme.

Her paper earned an A

(and a note from the teacher that said to keep writing!).

Gwendolyn Brooks

A

keep writing!

Soon, Gwendolyn headed off to college,
where she devoured thick books of poetry—
Dickinson, Wordsworth, and Hughes—
and penned poems about her family and friends.

After graduation, jobs were still hard to come by,
and poems didn't pay the bills.
So Gwendolyn found work wherever she could—
cleaning homes, typing, even making deliveries.

Then along came Henry,
a handsome man who adored poetry, too.
The two married and squeezed into a tiny apartment
in a Black neighborhood, where they were supposed to live.
A year later, baby Henry arrived.

A busy wife and mother,
Gwendolyn continued to write.
She took a poetry class at night,
where she studied modern poems
with different-length lines—
unpredictable meter and time.

Inspired, she created unique poems
about the nonstop busyness, the hard-luck grittiness,
of life in her South Side Chicago neighborhood—
Bronzeville—

where businesses boomed on 47th Street,
where hardworking families didn't have enough to eat,
where people jumped and jived to a new, jazzy beat.

And Gwendolyn kept polishing her words
until they sparkled like silvery summer clouds.

*"I am proud to feature people and their concerns—
their troubles as well as their joys."*

Eventually, one of her poems won a contest.
Then another. And another!
Some were published in a famous poetry journal.
But they still couldn't pay the bills.
Even without electricity, Gwendolyn kept writing by candlelight—
stories about life on her busy Bronzeville streets.

*"I wrote about what I saw
and heard in the street."*

And she kept dreaming
about a future that was going to be exquisite.

Then one day beneath a promising patch of clouds,
she gathered her finest poems—
stories of hardship and hope—
slid them into an envelope,
and mailed them to a book publisher in New York City.

NEGRO MEN
CAN CARRY
GUNS FOR
UNCLE SAM
SURELY
EY CAN DRI
MILK WAGO
FOR
WM.AN DAIR

Then she waited,
and worried,
and wondered,
would they like stories
about people in her neighborhood?

Soon a letter arrived.
The publisher wanted more—
twice as many as before.

So Gwendolyn composed poems in different forms.
Free verse. Ballads. Sonnets.
She wrote about brave soldiers like her brother,
fighting for a country
that didn't give everyone equal rights.
She wrote about a poor man
named Satin-Legs Smith,
who fancied fine clothes.
She wrote about understanding your identity—
who you are on the inside.
Her tired fingers wrote day and night
until finally
she had enough to send
to the publisher.

Before long, another letter arrived.
Gwendolyn grabbed that envelope,
ran into the bathroom, and locked the door.
Hands trembling, she opened it.
The publisher loved her poems!
Soon they became a beautiful book:
A Street in Bronzeville.

But Gwendolyn had more stories to share—
important stories
about a young girl growing up,
getting married, and starting her own family
in a city where people judged others by the color of their skin.
Those powerful poems became her second book, *Annie Allen*.

Gwendolyn's words d r i f t e d into the world
like bright, brilliant clouds.
Her poems helped people better understand others.
They encouraged people to take a closer look at themselves.
They changed the way some people thought and acted.

But even two books couldn't pay all the bills.
Money was tighter than ever.
Yet everywhere she looked,
Gwendolyn saw more stories that needed to be told.
So she kept writing.

Then one cloudy day in May,
Gwendolyn's electricity was turned off. Again.
Suddenly, the phone in her dark apartment started ringing.
Was it another bill collector?
She hesitated, then picked up the phone.
A reporter on the other end asked one question:
"Do you know that you have won the Pulitzer Prize?"

Gwendolyn couldn't believe it!
She grabbed her son
and danced around the apartment.

Outside,
exquisite clouds exploded in the sunset sky,
because Gwendolyn had won
the greatest prize in poetry!

Clouds (written by Gwendolyn Brooks at age fifteen)

Oh, when I look into the sky
And see those quiet clouds,
Now all arrayed in fleecy white,
Now dressed in colored shrouds,

It seems I cannot draw my eye
From that rich, heaven-land
And, drinking in the wide expanse,
I filled with rapture stand.

Unheedful of my transfixed state,
They float serenely by,
Those stately clouds
Calm sentries of the sky.

How can I fear to leave the earth
When heaven holds this glow!
Cloud-colored happiness and peace
Await me there, I know.

Author's Note

In 1950, Gwendolyn Brooks became the first Black person to win a Pulitzer when she won the Pulitzer Prize for Poetry for her second book, *Annie Allen*. Over the next five decades, she wrote fourteen more books, including a poetry book for children titled *Bronzeville Boys and Girls*. Gwendolyn often wrote about real-life topics that were important to her, such as love, loneliness, family, inequality, poverty, and war.

In her later years, Gwendolyn shared her passion for poetry by teaching writing classes at various colleges around Chicago. She also personally sponsored writing contests to help inspire young poets. In 1968, Gwendolyn was named the Poet Laureate of Illinois. She was appointed the Poet Laureate Consultant in Poetry to the Library of Congress in 1985—the first Black woman to hold that prestigious position.

Note: In her autobiography, Brooks stated she preferred the term "Black" instead of "African American." Her preference is reflected in this book.

Timeline

1917—Gwendolyn Elizabeth Brooks is born in Kansas on June 7, then moves to Chicago.

1924—She begins writing poems at age seven.

1928—Four of Gwendolyn's poems are published in the *Hyde Parker* newspaper.

1929—The Great Depression begins.

1930—*American Childhood* magazine publishes Gwendolyn's poem "Eventide."

1930—She attends Hyde Park High School.

1931—She attends Wendell Phillips Academy High School.

1932–34—She attends Englewood High School.

1934—Gwendolyn graduates from Englewood High School.

1936—Gwendolyn graduates from Woodrow Wilson Junior College (now known as Kennedy-King College).

1939—She marries Henry Blakely Jr. in her parents' home.

1940—Gwendolyn's son, Henry Blakely III, is born.

1941—Gwendolyn takes a local poetry class.

1943—She wins her first Midwestern Writers' Conference poetry contest.

1944—She wins her second Midwestern Writers' Conference poetry contest.

1945—She wins the combined Midwestern Writers' and Annual Writers' Conference poetry contest.

1945—Her first book, *A Street in Bronzeville*, is published.

1949—Her second book, *Annie Allen*, is published.

1950—Gwendolyn's book, *Annie Allen*, wins the Pulitzer Prize for Poetry.

1951—Gwendolyn's daughter, Nora Blakely, is born.

1953—Gwendolyn's third book, *Maud Martha*, is published.

1956—*Bronzeville Boys and Girls* is published.

1960—*The Bean Eaters* is published.

1968—Gwendolyn Brooks is named Poet Laureate of Illinois.

1972—Her first autobiography, *Report from Part One*, is published.

1985—Gwendolyn is appointed the Poet Laureate Consultant in Poetry to the Library of Congress.

1988—She is inducted into the National Women's Hall of Fame.

1994—She wins the National Book Foundation Medal for Distinguished Contribution to American Letters.

1996—Her second autobiography, *Report from Part Two*, is published.

2000—December 4: Gwendolyn Brooks passes away in Chicago.

Sources for Quotes

Page 7: "You are going to be the *lady* Paul Laurence Dunbar." Brooks, Gwendolyn. *Report from Part One*. Detroit: Broadside Press, 1972, p. 56.

Page 9: "I was at my happiest, sitting out on the back porch, to sit there and look out at the western sky with all those beautiful changing clouds and just to dream about the future, which was going to be ecstatically exquisite, like those clouds." Garland, Phyl. "Gwendolyn Brooks: Poet Laureate." *Ebony*, July 1968, p. 50.

Page 31: "I am proud to feature people and their concerns—their troubles as well as their joys." Brooks, Gwendolyn. *Report from Part One*. Detroit: Broadside Press, 1972, p. 135.

Page 32: "I wrote about what I saw and heard in the street." Watkins, Mel. "Gwendolyn Brooks, Whose Poetry Told of Being Black in America, Dies at 83." *New York Times*, December 4, 2000.

Page 40: "Do you know that you have won the Pulitzer Prize?" Gayles, Gloria Wade (ed.). *Conversations with Gwendolyn Brooks*. Jackson, MS: University Press of Mississippi, 2003, p. 33.

Page 48: "Poetry comes out of life." Brooks, Gwendolyn. "Interview." *TriQuarterly* magazine, Northwestern University, Spring/Summer 1984 issue (*Chicago*), no. 60, p. 409.

Select Bibliography

Alexander, Elizabeth (ed.). *The Essential Gwendolyn Brooks*. New York: Literary Classics of America, 2005.

Brooks, Gwendolyn. *Report from Part One*. Detroit: Broadside Press, 1972.

———. *Report from Part Two*. Chicago: Third World Press, 1996.

———. *Selected Poems: Gwendolyn Brooks*. New York: HarperCollins, 2006.

Garland, Phyl. "Gwendolyn Brooks: Poet Laureate." *Ebony*, July 1968.

Gayles, Gloria Wade (ed.). *Conversations with Gwendolyn Brooks*. Jackson, MS: University Press of Mississippi, 2003.

Kent, George E. *A Life of Gwendolyn Brooks*. Lexington, KY: University Press of Kentucky, 1990.

Melhem, D. H. *Gwendolyn Brooks: Poetry and the Heroic Voice*. Lexington, KY: University Press of Kentucky, 1987.

Watkins, Mel. "Gwendolyn Brooks, Whose Poetry Told of Being Black in America, Dies at 83." *New York Times*, December 4, 2000.

WTTW (Chicago-based public media organization). "From Riots to Renaissance: Bronzeville: The Black Metropolis." Access at: interactive.wttw.com/dusable-to-obama/bronzeville.

———. "From Riots to Renaissance: Jazz and Blues Music." Access at: interactive.wttw.com/dusable-to-obama/jazz-and-blues.

Acknowledgments

My sincere thanks to Siobhan McKissic and Anna Chen from the University of Illinois at Urbana–Champaign's Rare Book and Manuscript Library for granting access to Gwendolyn Brooks's precious handwritten poetry journals, and to Brooks Permissions for allowing us to share "Clouds," one of Ms. Brooks's priceless poems. —S.S.

A special thank you to the staff at the University of Illinois at Urbana–Champaign's Rare Book and Manuscript Library, where all of Ms. Brooks's personal papers are archived. Holding her handwritten papers and notebooks in my very hands was like her message in a bottle—so overwhelming and tender, it reverberates. Doing the research for the illustrations illuminated just how Gwendolyn Brooks overshadowed and transcended lack, limitation, oppression, and every established boundary line with the power of her discipline and the persistence of her love. Thank you, Gwendolyn Brooks. You speak still. —C.C.

"Poetry comes out of life."
—GWENDOLYN BROOKS

To Ginger, who adores children's books and her beautiful city of Chicago
—S.S.

To the living memory of Gwendolyn Brooks, who created wind
and an open door for millions of little poets
—C.C.

The illustrations in this book were made with acrylic paint.

Library of Congress Cataloging-in-Publication Data
Names: Slade, Suzanne, author. | Cabrera, Cozbi A., illustrator.
Title: Exquisite: the poetry and life of Gwendolyn Brooks / by Suzanne Slade; illustrated by Cozbi A. Cabrera.
Description: New York: Abrams Books for Young Readers, 2020.
Identifiers: LCCN 2018017974 | ISBN 9781419734113 (hardcover with jacket)
Subjects: LCSH: Brooks, Gwendolyn, 1917–2000—Juvenile literature. | Poets,
American—20th century—Biography—Juvenile literature. | African American
poets—Biography—Juvenile literature.
Classification: LCC PS3503.R7244 Z885 2018 | DDC 811/.54 [B]—dc23

Photograph of Gwendolyn Brooks on page 43 courtesy of
Library of Congress, Prints & Photographs division, LC-USZ62-107993

Text copyright © 2020 Suzanne Slade
Illustrations copyright © 2020 Cozbi A. Cabrera
Book design by Pamela Notarantonio

Printed and bound in China
10 9 8 7 6 5 4 3 2 1

Abrams Books for Young Readers are available at special discounts when purchased in quantity for premiums
and promotions as well as fundraising or educational use. Special editions can also be created
to specification. For details, contact specialsales@abramsbooks.com or the address below.

Abrams® is a registered trademark of Harry N. Abrams, Inc.

ABRAMS The Art of Books
195 Broadway, New York, NY 10007
abramsbooks.com